MY LIFE ON THE FARM
Mary Jo's Adventures
by
ANN AUBITZ

Ann Aubitz enjoys reading, writing short stories and spending time with her children. This book is very special to her, and near to her heart. It was written based on the stories told to her by her mother Mary.

Ann lives with her husband Brian and children; Christopher, Mitchell, Ashley and Katlyn. They reside in Bloomington, MN.

2013 by Ann Aubitz

ALL RIGHTS RESERVED… All images and text in this book have been reproduced with consent of the artists. No part of this book may be reproduced or transmitted in any form by any means, except as may be expressly permitted in writing from the publisher. Requests for permission should be addressed to:

Fuzion Print
1220 E 115th St
Burnsville MN 55337
www.fuzionprint.com
annaubitz@comcast.net

Historical Fiction

Edited by: Charlene Roemhildt

ISBN: 9780984461134

DEDICATED TO

This book is dedicated to my Mother. I cherish her fascinating stories and am in awe of the love her family had for one another through the toughest of times.

A special thanks to the wonderful women of WOW (Women of Words). I appreciate your support and encouragement more than you know. Also my deepest gratitude to my good friend Mary Jane.

And finally a HUGE thanks to my husband for putting up with my artistic whims and for printing this book.

UP FRONT

I have always been intrigued by my family history, but only recently have I come to realize how precious my Mother's stories truly are. At the time of printing my Mother Mary is the oldest sibling. She was born ninth in the family of sixteen, now there are only four remaining. She is currently 87 years old and remembers the stories as if they happened yesterday. The handwriting font is hers, so I may cherish it forever along with her stories.

I am so fortunate to still have her in my life, to tell me about the past. We eat lunch and I record her lovely memories. Each time I ask her how old she was she tells me six. So this is book is historical fiction. I am not sure of the exact order of the events, however, I am sure of the love this family felt for one another.

Ann Aubitz

FORWARD

Minnesotans living on farms in the 1930s hardly had a prosperous life. Quite the opposite—an agricultural depression dragged on for an entire decade. The men and women on these farms made enormous sacrifices to keep a roof over the family's head and food on the table.

This is a story of one such family as told by my mother, Mary Jo...

MY FINGER IN THE PUMP

Ouch! I still remember how much it hurt!

Chapter 1
My finger in the pump.

A Summer Day – 1932
Morrison County Township, Minnesota

"Come on Mary Jo Fussy, hurry up," Clara screamed at the top of her lungs. "Hold on to your pants," I yelled back at her, "My legs are shorter than yours." We ran though the tall grass by our large white wooden farm house. There were 11 of us kids in all with one more on the way.

I loved days like this. The sun shone brightly, birds sang, and there was not a cloud in the sky, not even the puffy kind. I was six years old that summer, the ninth child in the large Fussy brood.

"Mary Jo, what's takin' so long?" my older brother Robert asked, exasperated.
"I'm coming as fast as I can. The grass is too long." The grass was up to my shoulders as I struggled to keep up with my siblings.

As we neared the clearing by the water pump, I started skipping and twirling my beautiful new dress. It billowed out in the breeze behind me, making pretty shadows on the ground. My Mama had made the dress for me just that morning and I loved it. I knew the material came from a seed sack, but I didn't care. I would still be the prettiest girl at school, when I got to go to school, that is. It was a fine-looking dress, pale pink with bright blue flowers and a satin blue bow tied around my waist. Mama told me the blue in the material perfectly matched the color of my eyes.

I couldn't be happier that day—a beautiful summer day and a new dress, what could be better than this, I thought. The younger kids stopped running when they reached the water pump. They all took turns pumping the water. Pa used the pump to fill water basins so the cows and horses could drink. Now the pump was being used by us kids to get water and splash each other. The older kids knew better; Pa had told us all several times to stay away from the pump. My sisters and I jumped up on the concrete base of the huge black metal water pump anyway.

I got bored with the splashing and decided to climb to the very top of the pump.

"Mary Jo get down from there, you are going to crack your skull wide open," Clara said in a bossy tone.

I ignored Clara, and in one fluid motion I stuck my finger right in one of the holes on the pump. The minute I did it, I realized what a big mistake I had made. I quickly pulled my finger back, screaming.

The top layer of the skin of my finger was ripped clean off. All the kids ran to help me but it was too late. I knew my finger was bleeding, but I still tried to hide it behind my back as Mama came running toward me, the white towel in her hand waving in the wind. I guessed that one of my older brothers ran to get her and, of course, to tell on us.

I saw the look on Mama's face. She was furious with me and the other kids for messing around by the pump. We all knew there would be hell to pay later.

Looking up at Mama with huge tears in my eyes I held out my injured finger. Luckily Mama knew just how to take care of it; she gently inspected the skin and wrapped the clean towel around it. Mama said I was lucky my finger wasn't broken, but the skin was torn off.

The other kids took this opportunity to scatter away from Mama as fast as they could—the big chickens, I thought. We all knew she would go easier on them given some time.

When Mama and I were alone, I thought she would yell at me but all she did was gently take my hand and walk me back to our house.

THE PLACE WHERE JESUS SITS

or as mama would say

Miejsce, gdzie Jezus siedzi

Chapter Two
The place where Jesus sits

We strolled to the house hand-in-hand to get lunch ready for the workers. Once in the kitchen Mama gently lifted me up on the counter so I could help her cook. "Mary Jo, please put the peas in the pot for me," Mama said lovingly in her Polish dialect. I knew by lilt in her soft voice, that I was no longer in trouble for disobeying her and sticking my finger in the pump.

I never thought about it until I left the farm how unique my family actually was. Mama spoke Polish; Pa spoke German and all of us kids spoke English. The amazing thing about this is that we all understood each other. The only Polish we all spoke together was when we said our nightly prayers.

A smile comes to my face every time I think about Mama. She was an amazing cook. She would made fresh bread that would melt in your mouth. The bread would come out the oven and smell so delicious as mama sliced it. She would point to the hole on the inside of the loaf and say, "Miejsce, gdzie Jezus siedzi." This hole in the bread is the place where Jesus sits. She truly believed that Jesus blessed every morsel of food that passed over her table.

I didn't care for the farm animals much—the cows were so big they scared me and the chickens would peck at my feet. What I loved most of all was spending time in the kitchen with Mama. This was a special moment because with 11 kids, quiet moments alone with just me and Mama were rare.

Even though my finger still stung, I felt really special. I understood why Mama needed to be strict with us kids—the farm was a dangerous place. We all knew, deep down, that she was hard on us because she loved us and didn't want us to get hurt. We had all heard stories about kids who were maimed or killed on the farm because they played with equipment they shouldn't have.

As Mama prepared the workers' meal, I thought the great thing about her is that no matter what, she could always put good food on the table.

Mama had planted a large garden in an area that never grew anything. The soil was poor and sunlight was sparse. People often said that plants had no business growing in that awful soil. Yet Mama was able to plant cucumbers, beans, peas, and tomatoes and they all came out beautifully.

Mama never turned away a guest and always had enough food to give them bags of food on their way out the door. The neighbors all thought she was an angel because she always thought of her friends and family first. She was the first one up in the morning and the last one to go to bed at night. Everything she did was for her family and friends.

At a time when the entire world was in financial turmoil, we had a happy life on the farm. We kids were clueless about what was going on in the world outside the farm. We had everything we needed—a large simple farm house, a barn, and 70 acres of land for crops. The older kids like Clara Joe and Robert probably knew what was going on but at the time I rarely felt the effects of the Depression on the farm.

As I helped Mama prepare lunch, I ate a handful of peas right out of the pods. They were so fresh, the sweet flavor burst in my mouth. Mama put the peas I had just shelled on the wood-burning stove. Mama was cooking a chicken in one pot, while the potatoes and peas would go in the other two pots. This was how farm lunches were—big and plentiful so the farm workers had enough nourishment to last them until sundown.

I loved my big family; I loved the noise, the laughter and the friendship among my siblings. I miss it terribly now that most of them are gone. I knew that we truly loved each other and would do anything for our family.

After lunch everyone who was not going out to the fields stayed to clean up the mountain of dishes. Then we girls would go to pick eggs to get them ready to bring to market.

PICKING EGGS

Yuck the chickens are really smelly!

Chapter 3
Picking Eggs Yuck!

Chores on the farm were split up by gender. While the girls tended the garden and worked in the house, Pa and the older boys worked the farm. Pa would milk the cows, tend the fields, and raise pigs and chickens. He sold cream and milk at the local creamery, and eggs at the local market.

I sighed as I changed out of my pretty new dress and into my threadbare farm clothes so I could go pick eggs with my older sisters Irene and Clara. My work clothes were patched up so many times that patches were pretty much all that was left of my pants. I stuck my finger through a hole and wiggled it back and forth. "Mary Jo quit fussing about your pants. They are perfectly fine to go pick eggs.

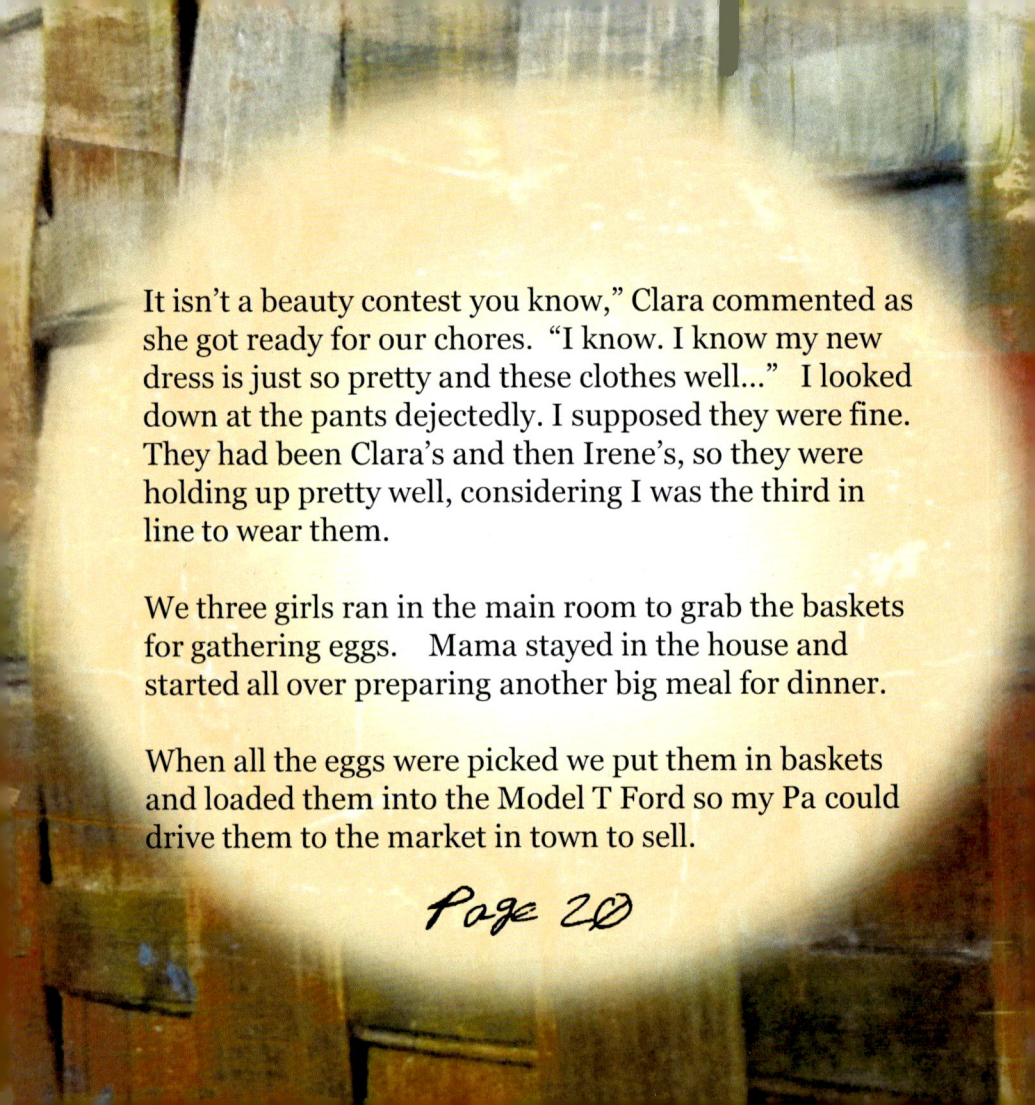

It isn't a beauty contest you know," Clara commented as she got ready for our chores. "I know. I know my new dress is just so pretty and these clothes well…" I looked down at the pants dejectedly. I supposed they were fine. They had been Clara's and then Irene's, so they were holding up pretty well, considering I was the third in line to wear them.

We three girls ran in the main room to grab the baskets for gathering eggs. Mama stayed in the house and started all over preparing another big meal for dinner.

When all the eggs were picked we put them in baskets and loaded them into the Model T Ford so my Pa could drive them to the market in town to sell.

Mama seldom picked the eggs, but she checked them to ensure that no broken eggs went to market. I remember the time Irene and I broke at least six eggs on the way from the coop to the house. Mama was so mad at us girls for wasting perfectly good eggs, we were sent to bed without supper.

I hated the chicken coop with all the noisy, messy, smelly chickens. So I would pick the eggs and run back to the house as fast as I could. That's why some of the eggs would occasionally break.

Irene and I finished in the coop, so I headed for the house, skipping from the coop to the house with the egg baskets swinging next to me.

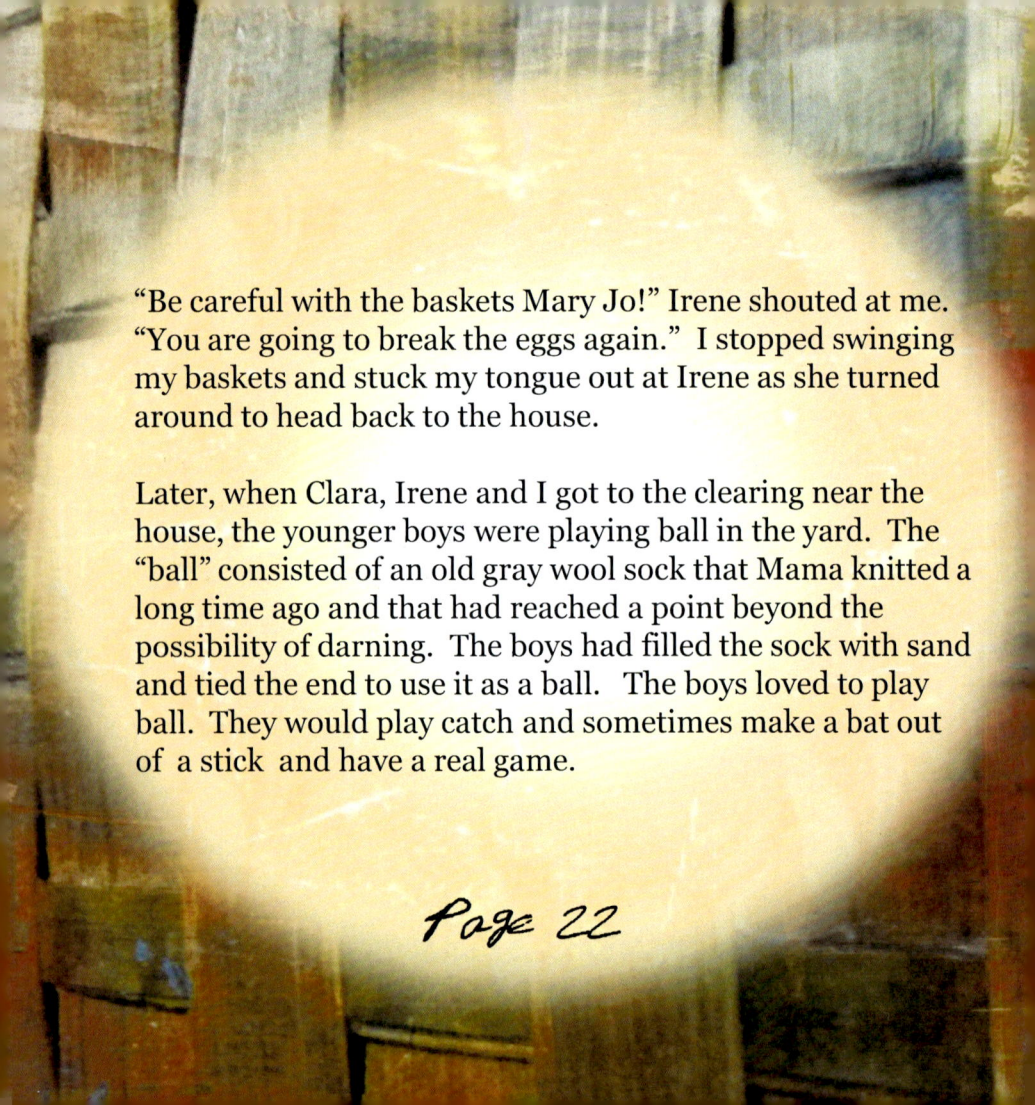

"Be careful with the baskets Mary Jo!" Irene shouted at me. "You are going to break the eggs again." I stopped swinging my baskets and stuck my tongue out at Irene as she turned around to head back to the house.

Later, when Clara, Irene and I got to the clearing near the house, the younger boys were playing ball in the yard. The "ball" consisted of an old gray wool sock that Mama knitted a long time ago and that had reached a point beyond the possibility of darning. The boys had filled the sock with sand and tied the end to use it as a ball. The boys loved to play ball. They would play catch and sometimes make a bat out of a stick and have a real game.

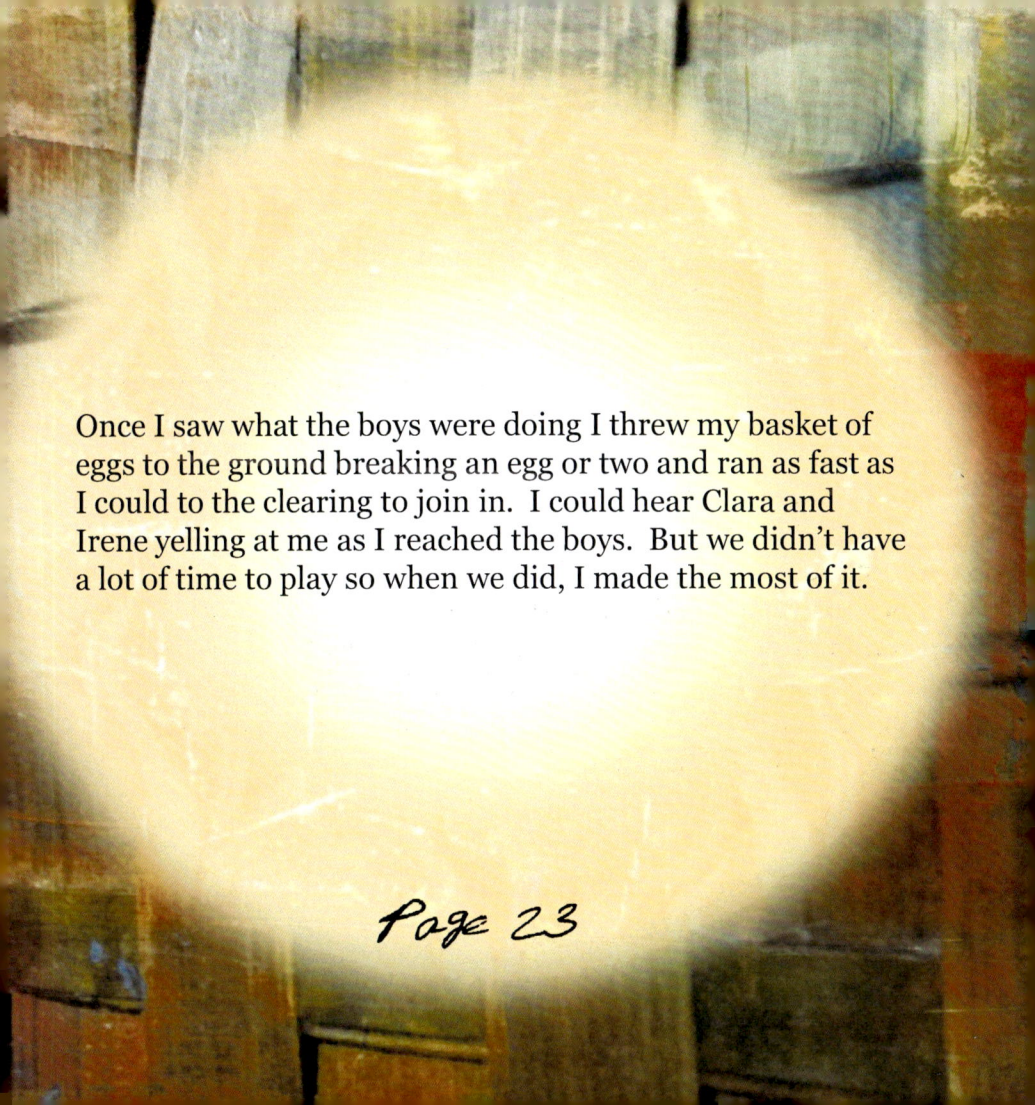

Once I saw what the boys were doing I threw my basket of eggs to the ground breaking an egg or two and ran as fast as I could to the clearing to join in. I could hear Clara and Irene yelling at me as I reached the boys. But we didn't have a lot of time to play so when we did, I made the most of it.

Hail Mary, full of grace. The Lord is with thee. Blessed art thou amongst women and blessed is the fruit of thy womb, Jesus. Holy Mary, Mother of God, pray for us sinners, now and at the hour of our death. Amen. Hail Mary, full of grace. The Lord is with thee. Blessed art thou amongst women and blessed is the fruit of thy womb, Jesus. Holy Mary, Mother of God, pray for us sinners, now and at the hour of our death. Amen. Hail Mary, full of grace. The Lord is with thee. Blessed art thou amongst women and blessed is the fruit of

HAIL MARY FULL OF GRACE

The Lord is with thee. Blessed art thou

Chapter 4
Hail Mary Full of Grace

We played ball in the yard until nightfall. That's when the workers came in from the fields and we kids got ready for bed.

Our house didn't have electricity, so we had lanterns to light our way up the stairs and into our attic. Robert, the oldest, lit the lantern, headed upstairs and motioned for the rest us to follow. It was a little spooky for me to head upstairs in the glow of the lantern, but I had the comfort of my family with me so it didn't bother me as much.

Mama and Pa followed us up the stairs and settled us in to our spacious room.

Ours was an old style farm house with a huge top floor where all us kids slept—three girls and eight boys. The girls slept on the small side of the attic and the boys slept on the larger side.

We each had a mattress and blankets that Mama made by hand. She used pedal sewing machine that she also used to make all the clothes for the family. She could quilt and crochet and always seemed to have time to do both. The house was a kaleidoscope of color and patterns—warm, comfy and homey.

Not only did mama make me that new pink dress with the blue flowers, but she also fixed my mattress. When the old one started to sag in the middle, Mama re-stuffed it with fresh straw and made a new blue and white stripped cover.

We put on our night clothes and all knelt near our mattresses to say our nightly prayers with Mama and Pa. Mama started praying the Hail Mary.

"Zdrowaś Maryjo, laski pełna Pan z Tobą, błogosławionaś Ty miedzy niewiastami błogosławiony owoc żywota Twojego, Jezus. Święta Maryjo, Matko Boża, módl się za nami grzesznymi teraz i w godzinę śmierci naszej. Amen."

Mama kissed each of us on the forehead and tucked the quilts up under our chins. I fell asleep breathing in the sweet smell of the new straw in my mattress.

As a child, I thought that everyone slept as soundly as I did, but I learned later that Mama and Pa spent sleepless nights worrying about the Depression. Another way of caring for us kids was to keep that worry from us. We always had food and they would feed the kids first, even if it was just a slice of bread.

SCHOOL DAYS

This is me! I am finally a big kid!

Chapter 5
I finally go to school

Today was the day! I was finally going to go to school; I woke up early, got my pretty school dress on and went down stairs before the others even woke. I sat at the table waiting for my day to start. I heard the first crow of the rooster in the yard and knew it was getting close to the time. This was it, the moment when I would be considered one of the big kids and go to school.

The others woke and came downstairs to find me at the kitchen table ready to go. Mama had gotten up a couple of minutes after me and started breakfast. I worked on setting the table, just like Mama taught me.

I was so nervous and excited that I hardly ate any of my breakfast. This morning Mama made scrambled eggs, bread from yesterday, and bacon from our last pig.

You would think that because we lived on a farm we would have meat all the time, but that was not the case. We were so thankful to have the meat on our table that morning we could hardly contain our excitement. A couple of months before, something really terrible had happened. We sent our prized pig to the butcher. The whole town knew that we were taking him in that day. The meat came back and we put it in our shed for storage. The next morning we woke to discover the entire pig had been stolen!

I had never seen Mama cry before. After Mama wiped her tears, she said softly "We will forgive these people for what they have done. They needed the food more than we did.," And that was the last word that was ever spoken about the stolen pig.

We all finished eating. The oldest boys Joe, Robert and Art, would stay home and work on the farm with Pa. Clara the oldest daughter, would take Irene, Roman, Clarence, Alfred, and me the mile and a half to our country school.

I couldn't contain myself—I skipped the whole way to school. The other kids followed behind me laughing and talking. "Don't fall down Mary Jo. You wouldn't want to get your pretty new dress all dirty," Clara declared from the back of the pack.

I slowed to look down at my new dress. I couldn't believe how lucky I was to get two new dresses in the last couple of weeks. I never got more than one new dress a year. This one was a beautiful pale green with white stripes.

After the first day I knew I would forever love attending school. Some of the other kids complained about the work, but I had a desire to learn. It was also exciting to get away from the farm and meet new people. We had great neighbors across the road that we played with as much as we could, yet it was still nice to meet different people.

When school was over for the day we gathered in the school yard for our long walk home. Other kids got to take the bus to and from school, but for some reason our family had to walk. Thinking back, we only rode the bus one time in all the years we lived at this farm. After passing us day after day walking in horrible weather, the bus driver had pity on us on one extremely frigid Minnesota day and stopped to pick us up. It was the first time I had ever been in a bus.

I fondly remember my parents being very supportive about all of us going to school. Many kids in our area were not as lucky. They had to work the farm when the family needed it, which was most of the time. With so many children in our family, the younger kids could attend school often. I cherished the experience and held on to the love of learning throughout my life.

THRESHING

thresh
v. **threshed, thresh·ing, thresh·es**
v.tr.
1.
a. To beat the stems and husks of (grain or cereal plants) with a machine or flail to separate the grains or seeds from the straw.
b. To separate (grains or seeds) in this manner.
2. To discuss or examine (an issue, for example) repeatedly.
3. To beat severely; thrash.
v.intr.
1. To use a machine or flail to separate grain or seeds from straw.
2. To thrash about; toss.

Chapter 6
Threshing Machine Fire

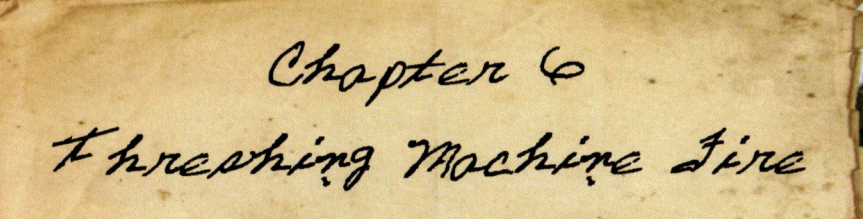

In the autumn, after the grain had ripened in the shocks, it was ready to be threshed so Pa could sell it in town.

The threshing process in the past was done by removing it from the stalks by hand.., When I was growing up, it this was accomplished by a threshing machine. I hated the large noisy equipment. Luckily, for me at least, our farm was not large enough or wealthy enough to own one of those dreaded threshing machines. Since we couldn't afford one ourselves, Pa would rent the machine and hire men to do the threshing for him. Threshing required a huge amount of labor and time. I remember the crew being on our property for a week or more.

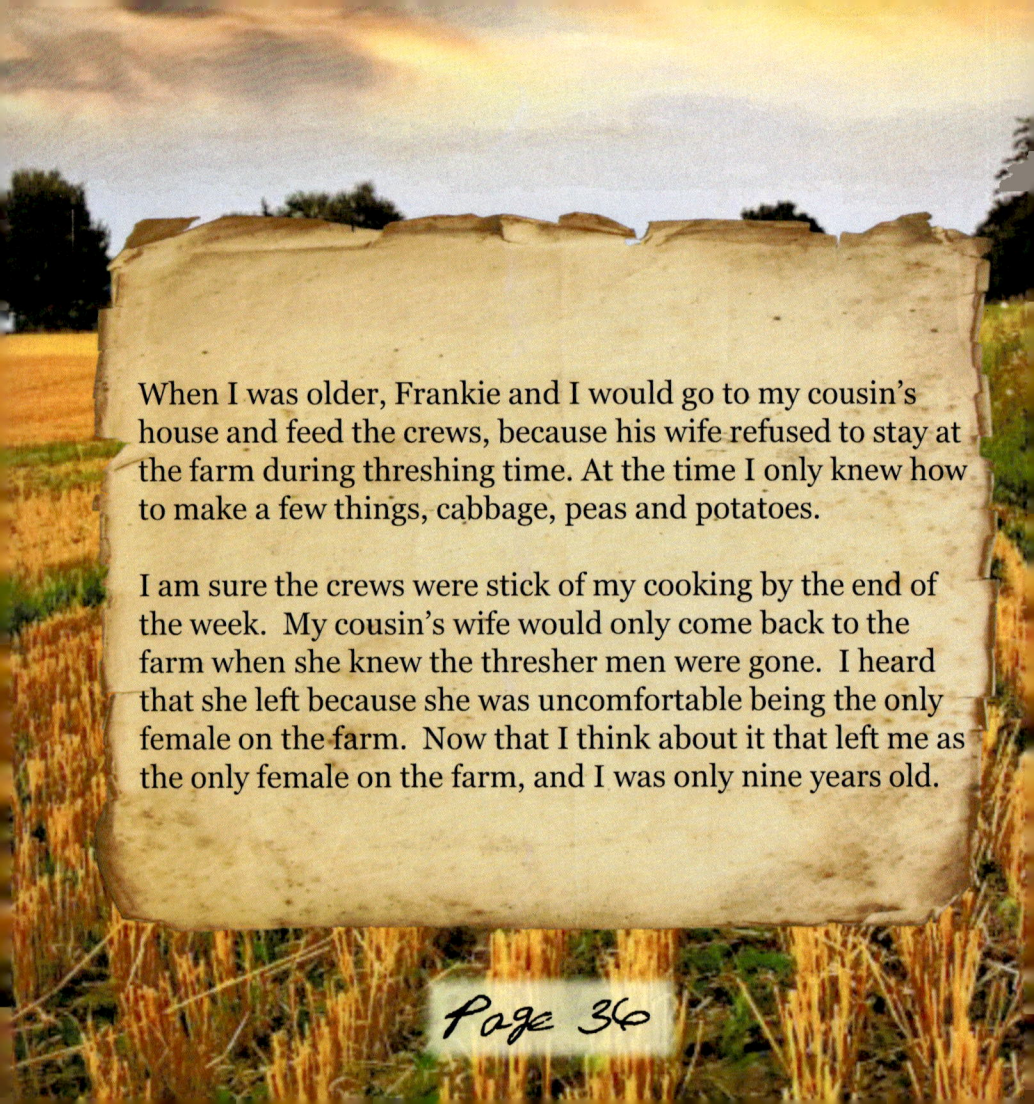

When I was older, Frankie and I would go to my cousin's house and feed the crews, because his wife refused to stay at the farm during threshing time. At the time I only knew how to make a few things, cabbage, peas and potatoes.

I am sure the crews were stick of my cooking by the end of the week. My cousin's wife would only come back to the farm when she knew the thresher men were gone. I heard that she left because she was uncomfortable being the only female on the farm. Now that I think about it that left me as the only female on the farm, and I was only nine years old.

In the summer of my sixth year the harvest was the earliest in Minnesota history. Pa contacted the crew and soon the threshing machine was started. Men stood on top of the wagon and pitched the grain bundles down into the threshing machine's bundle feeder. We all watched from the yard as the big machine huffed and puffed. It was my least favorite thing on the farm, because it was so big and noisy.

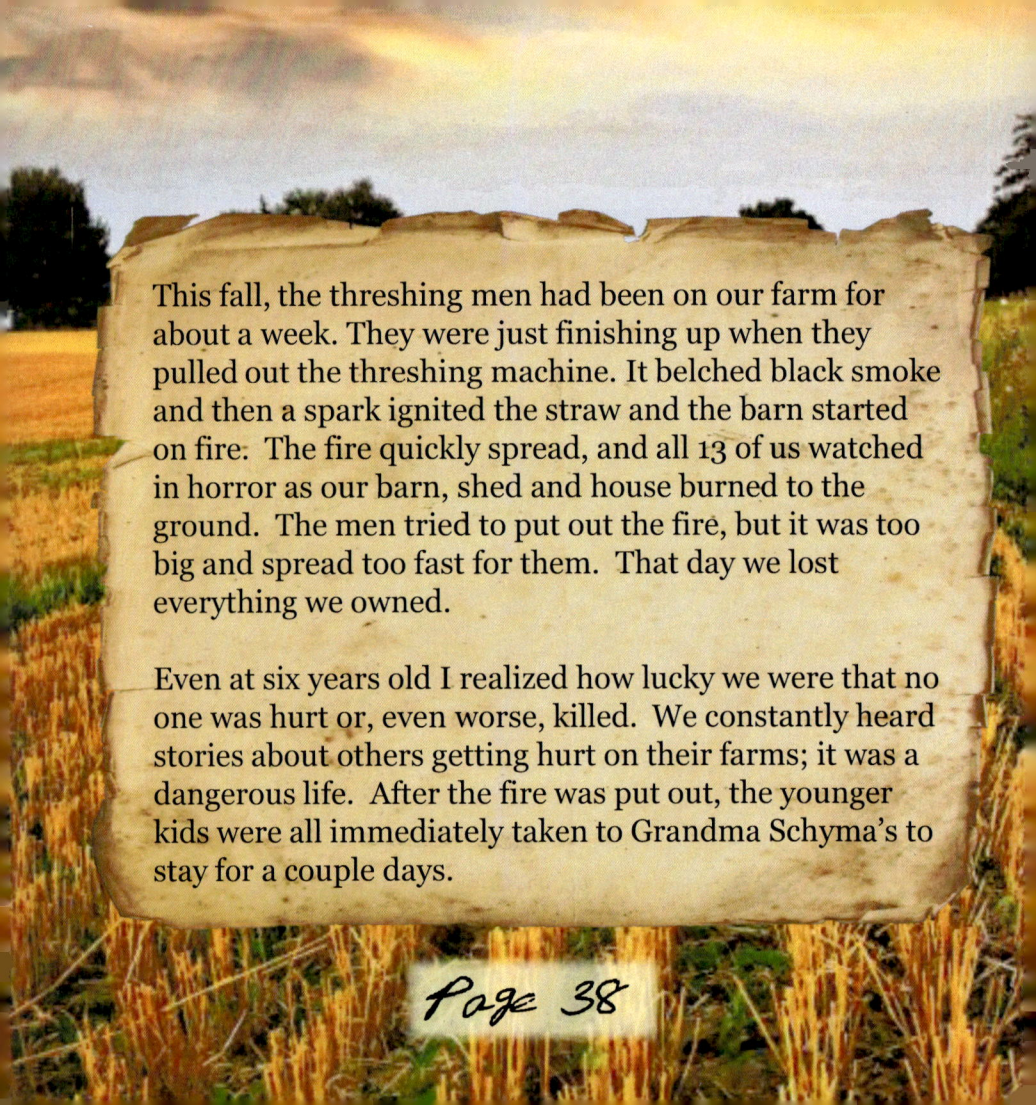

This fall, the threshing men had been on our farm for about a week. They were just finishing up when they pulled out the threshing machine. It belched black smoke and then a spark ignited the straw and the barn started on fire. The fire quickly spread, and all 13 of us watched in horror as our barn, shed and house burned to the ground. The men tried to put out the fire, but it was too big and spread too fast for them. That day we lost everything we owned.

Even at six years old I realized how lucky we were that no one was hurt or, even worse, killed. We constantly heard stories about others getting hurt on their farms; it was a dangerous life. After the fire was put out, the younger kids were all immediately taken to Grandma Schyma's to stay for a couple days.

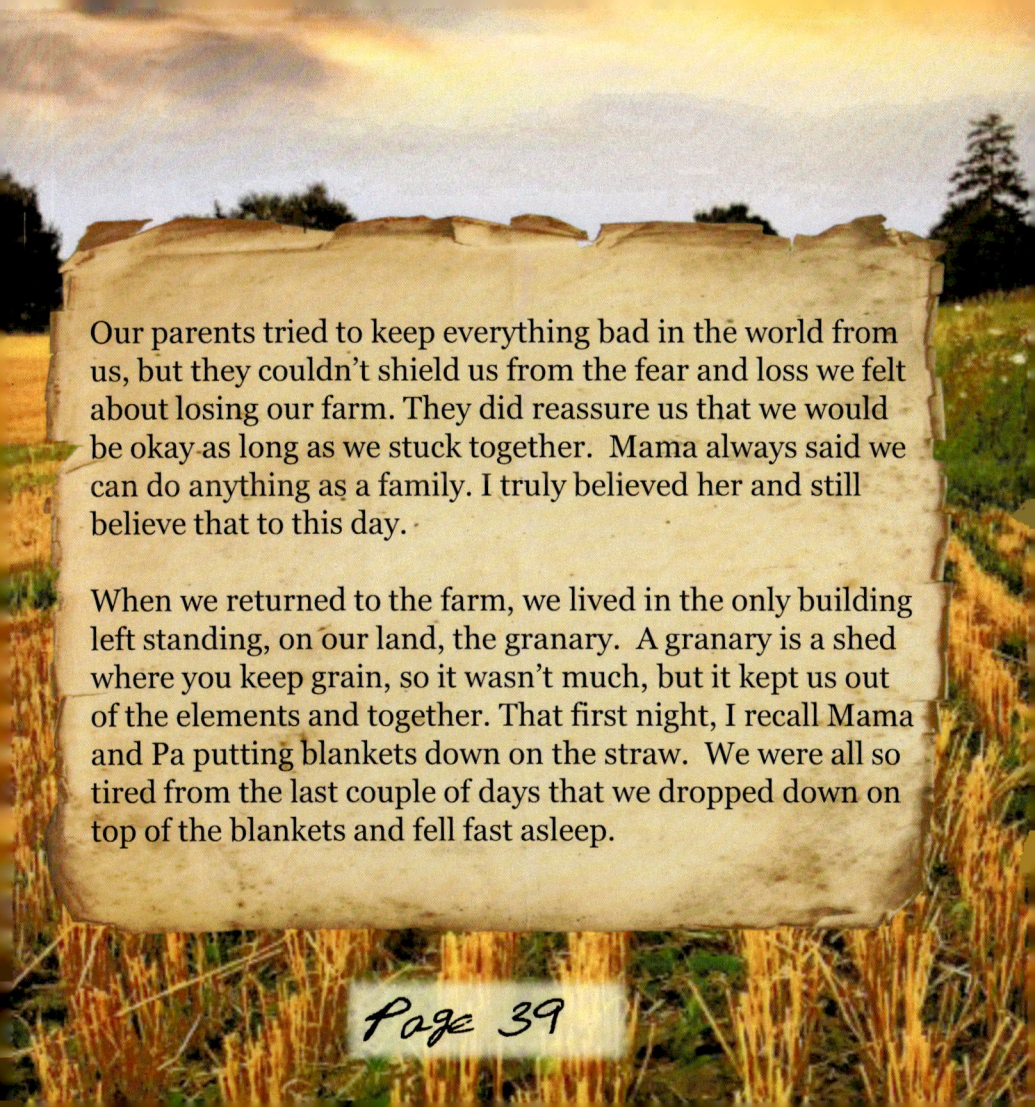

Our parents tried to keep everything bad in the world from us, but they couldn't shield us from the fear and loss we felt about losing our farm. They did reassure us that we would be okay as long as we stuck together. Mama always said we can do anything as a family. I truly believed her and still believe that to this day.

When we returned to the farm, we lived in the only building left standing, on our land, the granary. A granary is a shed where you keep grain, so it wasn't much, but it kept us out of the elements and together. That first night, I recall Mama and Pa putting blankets down on the straw. We were all so tired from the last couple of days that we dropped down on top of the blankets and fell fast asleep.

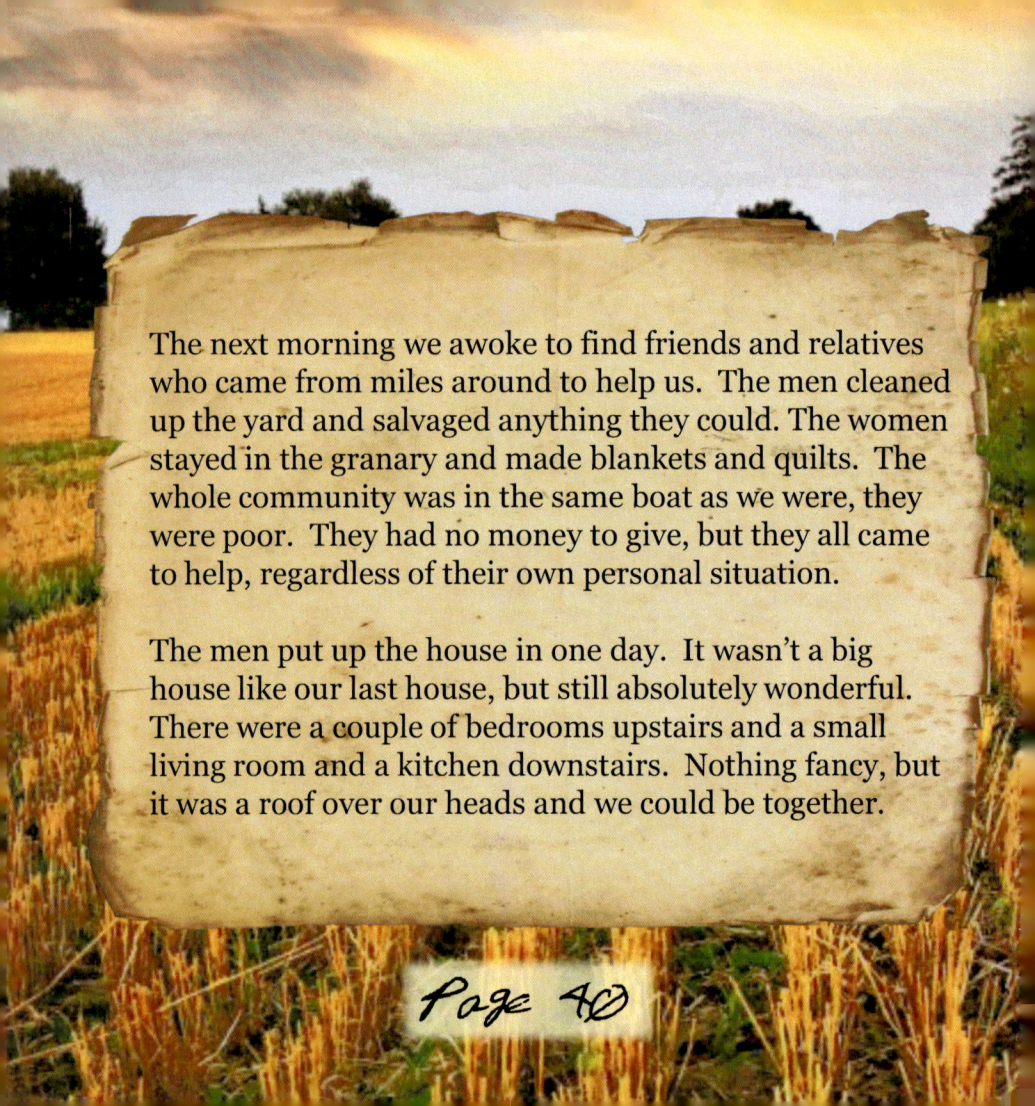

The next morning we awoke to find friends and relatives who came from miles around to help us. The men cleaned up the yard and salvaged anything they could. The women stayed in the granary and made blankets and quilts. The whole community was in the same boat as we were, they were poor. They had no money to give, but they all came to help, regardless of their own personal situation.

The men put up the house in one day. It wasn't a big house like our last house, but still absolutely wonderful. There were a couple of bedrooms upstairs and a small living room and a kitchen downstairs. Nothing fancy, but it was a roof over our heads and we could be together.

As we were moving in to our new home, Mama stopped us all and said a prayer. "We are blessed that we have so many people that love and care for us. May God thank them for their selflessness and may His glory shine on us in our new home. Amen."

Little did we know that our time in our new home was fleeting.

I will ever miss the barn!

GOODBYE FARM

Chapter 7 – Goodbye Farm

I woke up with chills and realized how cold the attic felt. The rest of the kids were still sleeping. I guess the cold didn't bother them as much. We kids knew what it felt like to be cold;, Minnesota winters were and still are brutal. Sometimes the temperature got down to 20 or 30 below zero.

But to me, the attic felt particularly cold this morning. I put on my clothes and ran downstairs to look out a window. They were all fogged on the inside from the cold. I ran my hand across the pane and peered through the smudge I had made on the window. The snow was all the way up to the window sill, so it was hard to see the yard. Judging by the drifts, the snow would be up to my shoulders. It had been snowing for the last two days, but I did not expect this much. It was like a frozen wonderland.

We wouldn't be going anywhere today! I loved days like this, all of us together, hanging around the fireplace trying to keep warm. We all grabbed our blankets and quilts from our beds and wrapped up tight. Mama made us warm milk and sweet bread as a treat. I hoped we would get to go outside to play today with our friends. The neighbor kids lived across the road from my family for as long as any of us could remember; they were like an extended part of our family.

I knew Mama and Pa would not rest today. Mama would be cooking and baking. Pa always had chores outside. The night before, I had heard Mama and Pa talking about him going to Little Falls today to pay the deed to the house. Pa came in the living room to fetch my older brother Robert and said that it was time to go to Little Falls, because he had the money to pay off the farm. Pa and Robert walked outside, but that deep snow was just too much for our Model-T. No matter what they tried, they couldn't get the car out of the driveway.

Before dawn the next day, Robert pushed the car out of the driveway while Pa steered. Pa and Robert miraculously made it to the bank in Little Falls only to find out that another family swooped in and bought our farm out from under us. The other family (who shall remain nameless) figured that Pa would not make it to town in the storm, so they stayed in a hotel in Little Falls and were at the bank first thing in the morning.

This was another devastating blow to the family. Mama and Pa had lived in the house for a long time; every single child had been born in this home, including me. I would miss our farm, and once again Mama and Pa reassured us that everything would be okay, but I wasn't so sure this time...

COWS IN THE ROAD

What a sight!

Chapter 8 – Cows in the road
Morrill to Gilman

Thinking back on the experience, I'm sure we were a sorry sight!

I was so sad that we had to move from our home in Morrill (Morrison County Township) to Gilman, but the sight of us walking down the road with our 60 or so cows still makes me laugh to this day. The older boys walked down the road with the cows while the younger kids sat in the car.

It took two weeks to pack up the house— they gave us until spring to find a new place to live. Meanwhile, Pa and Mama had thought up every possible scenario, but it was difficult to find a place to live that would house 12 kids. It was decided that we would move in with relatives until we could find a place of our own to rent. We were in enough financial trouble it was impossible to buy a home at this time. The cows we had were not producing much milk and now that we didn't have the farm, the older boys didn't have work. There just wasn't enough money to support the whole family. Joe hopped on a train the next week and headed out West. Art, Clarence and Roman headed to the Dakotas to find work.

I loved having our family together and was terribly sad when they all left. A my age, I did not understand why the boys had to leave.

We stayed with relatives for a couple of weeks, then moved into a big beautiful house in Gilman. I found out later that the guy lived there was a little bit on the outside of the law. He was a truck driver, so he was never at the house so he could rent it to us. The house was absolutely gorgeous, but the weird thing was that he ruined a beautiful porch by cutting it out so he could hide his entire truck in the back of the house. It would have been grea to have all that room for our family.

I loved so many things about going to school in Gilman, even though it lasted a short time. The walk wasn't nearly as far from our old house to the school. The teacher was nice, and so much fun. He was not only the teacher, but also owned the general store. When he found out we were leaving Gilman for Granite Ledge, he sent us to his store to get snacks and items to have a going away party.

Heading into our new life... Granite Ledge

LEAVING GILMAN FOR OUR NEW LIFE IN GRANITE LEDGE

Chapter 9
Granite Ledge

We rented the house in Gilman for only a couple of months. Pa found property to purchase in Granite Ledge. He raised the money by selling all his cows at auction, getting relief checks from the government and using money Art, Clarence and Roman were able to send back to us. This was the only way we would be able to afford a new house and barn. We didn't have land or animals any more, but it was a nice house that was perfect for our family.

The greatest thing about Granite Ledge was the school was only a block away! I loved the fact we didn't have to walk the mile and a half to school anymore. The general store was next to the school, so it was great for Mama. Although Pa was not farming his own land, he could work on other people's farm for money.

We lived in Granite Ledge for a few years, and then I left the farm to work for my aunt and uncle in their store.

This was only one year in our lives. It was such a tough year, but at the same time one of the greatest times of my life. I love my family and cherish memories of them and our times growing up. I think of them often and miss them terribly.

My Photo Album

Pa and Mama 1911

My Photo Album

Clara

My oldest sister Clara. I loved Clara so much. When I was 16 she was very sick. I moved in to take care of her and her kids. She left this world way too soon!

My Photo Album

Joe

Joe was my oldest brother. I will never forget the day he hopped on a train and left the farm. He ended up in Montana then Nevada.

My Photo Album

Robert

Robert loved working on the farm with Pa. He became a wonderful farmer.

My Photo Album

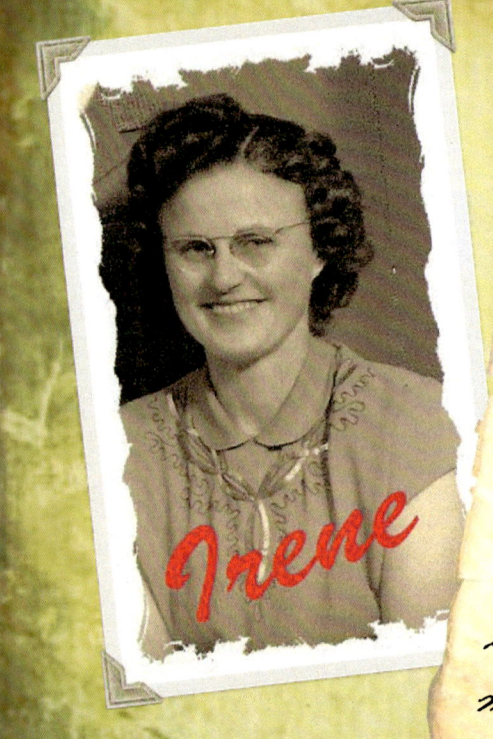

Irene

Irene and I did everything together on the farm. We lived by each other when we were older and were lucky enough to spend much time together.

My Photo Album

Art

Art and I were great friends from the start and it continued on late into our lives. I cherished the times I got to speak with him on the phone and will miss his wonderful stories.

My Photo Album

Roman

This is a photo of me and Roman before he left the farm to find work

My Photo Album

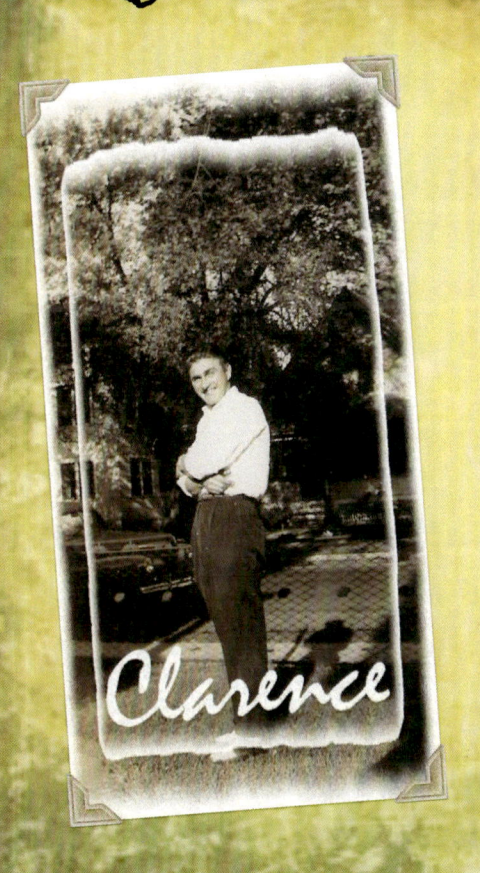

Clarence

Clarence was always one of my best friends, not only as kids but in to our adult years as well.

My Photo Album

Alfred joined the military then spent his entire life farming not far from where we grew up.

Alfred

Circa-1940

My Photo Album

The photo below is one of my favorites, the other one is not, I hate that I am in my work coveralls.

4 years old - 1940

Mary

This was taken in 1945

My Photo Album

Frank

Frankie was closest to me as we were growing up. We worked together so we spent a lot of time together. Photo circa 1942

My Photo Album

Lawrence and I went to school together through the years. I still talk to him as much as I can.

Lawrence

My Photo Album

Gertie

Gertie lived in Minnesota for a while then married and moved to Oregon where she lived out her life. Photos circa 1945

My Photo Album

Bill

Bill ended up leaving the farm after he had grown and moved to the cities. We spoke often and had many great times together.

My Photo Album

Jerome

Jerome was killed working on a train when he was 18 years old. It was a terrible time for our family.

My Photo Album

Richard

Richie is the youngest boy in the family. He still picks on me like he did when he was a kid.

My Photo Album

Delores

Delores is the baby of the family. She has not changed much in all these years. She is still pretty as ever.

My Photo Album

My lovely sisters.
Irene, Clara, Me
Delores, Gertie
Around 1942

My Photo Album

Nine of my brothers
photo taken in the 1950's
Robert, Alfred, Art, Lawrence, Bill, Frank,
Jerome, Richard, and Joe

My Photo Album

This is all of us. The photos were taken from two different pictures from two different family gatherings — we never had a family photo taken with all 18 of us present.

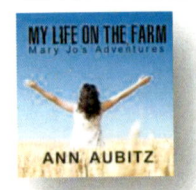

TO PURCHASE
MY LIFE ON THE FARM

Mary Jo's Adventures
Contact the Author
Ann Aubitz
annaubitz@comcast.net
952.465.2623
http://ann615.wix.com/mylifeonthefarm